THE PAST IN PICTURES

A further collection of photographs of the London Borough of Sutton over the last century

Compiled by June Broughton

Design: Shirley Edwards

London Borough of Sutton Libraries and Arts Services

Introduction

This volume, like its predecessor, "All Our Yesterdays", reproduces a selection of photographs taken from the illustrations collection in the Local Studies section of the Central Library. This collection has been built up over the years by the kindness of individuals, who donate pictures, or lend photographs for copying. Their concern, like ours, is that these reminders of our past should not be lost, but preserved for posterity.

Only occasionally does a really big haul of hitherto unknown material come our way. This happened in 1977, when we acquired, through the generosity of Linwood Strong, a large collection of glass plate negatives from the cellar of their shop in Sutton High Street. They proved to be the work of David Knights Whittome, a photographer to George V, who occupied the shop from 1905 to 1916. Many of the plates were insufficiently identified, or too badly damaged to print, but from this collection we have been able to add a good many new pictures to our stock. A number of these prints appear in this book.

Acknowledgements

I acknowledge, with grateful thanks, the help of my colleagues Douglas Cluett and Shirley Edwards; and of George Jenkinson, for reproducing photographs with great skill and speed. To Frank Burgess special thanks are due; not only for his historical and photographic advice on this volume, but for his work on the Knights Whittome plates, to which he gave much time, trouble and expert attention. His work is hereby gratefully acknowledged.

First published 1981

© London Borough of Sutton Libraries and Arts Services
Central Library, St. Nicholas Way, Sutton, Surrey. Tel. 01-661 5050

ISBN 0 907335 03 9

Printed by John Bentley (Printers) Ltd., Todmorden. A member of the Dunn & Wilson Group Ltd.

Charter Day procession, 12th September 1934. On that day, Sutton & Cheam received the Charter promoting it from an urban district to a borough. On the corner of Throwley Road is the former well-known landmark, Joe Lyons, and on the right is Boots' old shop.

Boorne's Brewery House, London Road, Wallington, c.1870. The Brewery premises lay behind the house, and to the right of it, as viewed in this photograph; the entrance to it was between the fence on the right and the house. To the left is the house of the brewery foreman, almost a smaller copy of the employer's house.

James Boorne and his wife, Amelia. James inherited the Brewery in 1848, marrying Amelia, then a widow with three children, in 1857. This picture is a typical formal Victorian photograph, with James clutching the family Bible and Amelia presumably in her Sunday best.

"Cyclist Rest", Wallington Corner

Wallington Corner at the beginning of the century, showing the Cyclists' Rest, now a newsagent's shop. Tucked around the corner, to the right of the Cyclists' Rest in this view, is the Rose & Crown, a tied house to Boorne's Brewery until 1927. The road passing in front of the Rose & Crown is Butter Hill. To the right, London Road leads off between the wall of Wallington Manor House on the right, and Elm Grove opposite.

Carshalton's first tram, 1906, and a gathering of local residents. This photograph was probably taken at the depot in Westmead Road. The line ran from West Croydon to the terminus at The Grapes, Sutton. The fare for the entire journey was 3½d.

Carshalton Fire Brigade, Pound Street, in the 1890s. The Fire Station was built in 1867 to house a new engine, for which a properly organised Brigade of Volunteers was formed. In this group the white-bearded man at the front is Chief Fire Officer Harwood. The man standing on the engine with his hand on his belt is his second-in-command, Mr. Woolgar. The dog, complete with muzzle, belongs to Mr. Harwood.

Wallington Public Library and gardens, soon after opening in 1936. The upper storey of the Library was added in 1962–3. The site of the tennis courts on the right, across Shotfield, is now occupied by the Magistrates Court.

Official opening of the Town Hall, Wallington, on 21st September 1935. It was built on the site of a house called 'Sunny Bank', which had been used by several Council departments before being demolished in 1934 to make way for the new building.

ST. ANTHONY'S

St. Anthony's Hospital, North Cheam, c.1913, in the building that had been the Lord Nelson Inn. This became a nurses' home when the new hospital was built in 1914.

The Hospital built in 1914, pictured c.1930. It was demolished in 1978 to make way for the present complex of buildings.

HOSPITAL

St. Anthony's Hospital: patients undergoing a 'fresh air cure' in 1910.

Wandle Mills at Butter Hill Bridge, in 1896. On the left is Ansell's Snuff Mill, which ceased to operate in 1896. Its large old water-wheel was demolished in 1912, but its buildings, no longer weather-boarded, still exist, though scheduled for demolition. On the right is Denyer's Flour Mill. This building has been replaced by a modern one.

H. Skipp, farrier and blacksmith, Wandle Road, Beddington, c.1905. Mr. Skipp, who became a Sergeant Farrier in World War I, is on the right, next to his brother Tom. The two little Skipps are Sam and Philip.

The name-board proclaims: "Horses shod carefully on improved principles."   (This picture forms part of the cover design)

Sutton Public Hall in 1900. The lamp columns have survived to the present day, although the lamps themselves have gone. The fire escape hut contained the firemen's collapsible ladder, and the fire pump was housed beneath the stage, entering through a door further down the slope on the left. The building is due to be demolished this year (1981) and the site redeveloped.

Sutton Municipal Offices in 1902 soon after the building was completed. It stood in the High Street, on the corner of Throwley Road, until it was demolished in 1970.

Sutton Arcade, High Street, c.1927. The Arcade was built by Mr. Ernest Shinner, whose shop is on the left of the picture, in 1926. The uniformed commissionaire kept order and locked the collapsible gates at closing time.

Derby day traffic at the Duke's Head, Wallington Green, in 1918. This photograph was taken by Mr. Horace Webber, whose shop can be seen projecting beyond the pub.

The Ponds, Carshalton, early this century. Until the 1820s, when the road to the south of the ponds and the bridge across them were built, carts had to splash through the ponds in both directions, though pedestrian footways existed. It was a common occurrence for carts to get stuck in the mud. Nevertheless, as this picture shows, the north-south ford continued to be used long after the bridge was built.

Second World War bomb damage, Wallington Green. Mr. Webber's bootmaker's & mender's shop, which stood next to the Duke's Head, was hit on the evening of February 20th, probably 1941. Because it was their daughter's birthday, the Webbers were visiting her when the bomb landed on their home. The site is now occupied by the pub's car park.

St. Philomena's class, 1907. This splendid photograph, from a Knights Whittome plate, reveals a patriotic pyramid of pupils during what would nowadays, presumably, be a gymnastics lesson.

Sports day, St. Philomena's, 1908. School and visitors gather on the lawn, and watch intently as pupils compete in a ladylike tug-of-war.

St. Philomena's, Carshalton, 1908. Pupils boat on the lake, which was one of the sources of Carshalton Ponds and the River Wandle. It is now dry, except when the water table is exceptionally high. The water tower, built by Sir John Fellowes, supplied piped water to the house, a rare luxury in the 18th century. The Daughters of the Cross bought Carshalton House in 1893 and have run a school there ever since.

Procession past the Queen's Head, Mill Green Road, Beddington Corner, c.1910. Taking part are the Beddington Corner Band and the Volunteer Fire Brigade, plus the two smartly stepping figures in top hat and bowler. Little is known of the band, though it may have been formed from mill-workers employed in the various local mills on the Wandle.

The Red Lion, Hackbridge Road, Hackbridge, c.1920. The pub is an eighteenth century building, although the interior has been much altered. Members of the Clark family were licensees from 1905 until Mr. Dennis Clark's retirement in 1979. The cottages beyond the pub may have been built by the sons of Admiral Sir Benjamin Hallowell-Carew of Beddington Park.

Tram depot, Westmead Road, Carshalton, c.1910. The trams are standing over inspection pits. The sheds are still in existence, used by a private firm. This photograph was produced from a Knights Whittome glass negative.

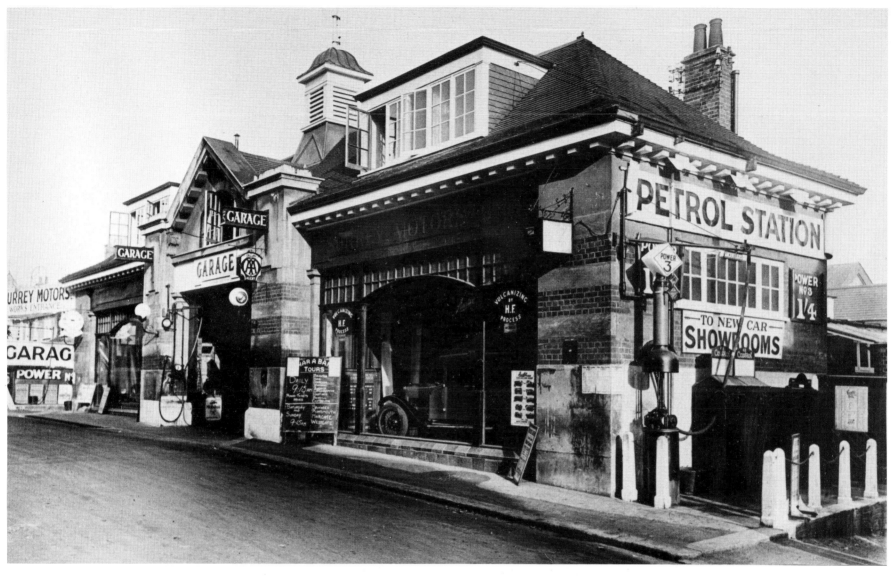

Speedway House, Surrey Motors building in St. Nicholas Road, in the 1920s. The garage was built in 1912, and taken over by Surrey Motors in 1919. It was demolished in 1961 when St. Nicholas House was built. Surrey Motors was taken over by Epsom Coaches in 1979.

Mr. Short's Dairy, Grove Road, Sutton, about 1915. The sign on the window tells us: "Pure milk from our Westmead Farm Dairy, Shorts Road, Carshalton, established 1841". The right-hand window is inscribed: "Inspection of cowsheds invited".

Mr. Short's milk cart, 1917. Jessie and Charlotte Taylor, pictured here, took over from Mr. Richmond, who went for war service. Most customers had cans for milk, though a few better-off people had bottles.

Gardner's saddler's shop, High Street, with its original Georgian shop front, in about 1870. The building on the right is the old Red Lion, which stood to the south of the present pub.

LAMBERT'S

The manufacture of snuff was an industry carried out locally in mills powered by the River Wandle. At the turn of the century Alexander Lambert's snuff mill at Hackbridge produced up to five tons of snuff a week. These pictures of the processes in snuff-making were taken at Lambert's mill for a magazine article published in 1900.

Traditional method: 2 upright wheels revolve on a granite bedstone to grind the snuff.

OLD AND NEW METHODS OF GRINDING SNUFF IN USE AT ONE AND THE SAME TIME

New method: mechanical pestles roll in their mortars to grind the snuff into a fine powder.

24

SNUFF MILL

A snuff-drying oven.

This photograph was captioned: "After forty years – a snuff-and-sneeze-proof man".

A publicity shot – a workman weighed against bags of snuff.

25

The Plough, Sutton Common Road, in 1912. A modern building replaced this cottage-style pub, which stood near the intersection of Sutton Common Road and Sutton By-pass, but was bombed in October 1940. The present pub was built in 1959, on a site behind the old building pictured here.

Surrey staghounds in Carshalton Park, probably taken in the 1870s or 1880s. A herd of deer was kept in the park for the Surrey Hunt, and tended by Mr. Puttock, the deer-keeper, who lived in a cottage in The Square.

The Pond, Carshalton.

Lower Pond, Carshalton, c.1910. The tile roof between the trees stands in front of Woodman's butcher's shop. Beneath it, carcasses were hung on display. The shop, which dates from at 'least the 16th century, is next to All Saints Church, and may have been a priest's house. It is now a wine bar.

Carshalton Road, Sutton.

Carshalton Road, Sutton, about 1917. On the left is the Jenny Lind, named after the popular singer who was known as the 'Swedish nightingale'. She is said to have sung from a balcony when visiting friends nearby. Nalder & Collyer were brewers in Croydon.

28

Old Cottage, Malden Road, Cheam, pictured in 1922, just before it was dismantled to facilitate road widening. It was reconstructed on its present site, set back and further along from its position here. A milk cart stands in front of the cottages on the right, which were demolished in 1932.

High Street, Carshalton, c.1913. The London & Provincial Bank began its operations in Carshalton Hall, moving into these premises on the corner of The Square in 1898. The shop next to the bank is Ridley's grocer's and wine merchant's, which served the area for many years. The trees of Carshalton Park can be seen at the end of the row of shops on the left-hand side of the road.

The Odeon, Central Road, Worcester Park, just before it closed in 1956, after 22 years. The building is now an International supermarket (1981).

The Odeon, Wallington, showing "A Queen is Crowned" in 1953, to parties of schoolchildren. The Odeon, which stood on the corner of Woodcote Road and Ross Parade, was opened in 1934 and closed in the early 1960s. The building is now a supermarket.

Sutton Picture Theatre, Cheam Road, Sutton, in 1928, showing Syd Chaplin in "The man on the box". It opened in 1911, advertising that at matinees, teas, coffee and ices would be served free. In 1953 it became The Curzon and in 1971 was converted to Studio 1,2,3.

One of a series of cards showing the High Street in Christmas Show Week, 1910. On the right stand Mr. Shinner's two shops, and the Baptist Church, which he acquired and demolished in 1934, in order to expand up to the corner of Hill Road. On the left is the Bio-Picture Hall, on the corner of the Arcade, a short-lived venture, held in the shop basement.

High Street, Sutton, in c.1930. On the right is the Surrey County Cinema, which opened in 1921. It subsequently became the Gaumont, which survived until 1959. A W. H. Smith branch now stands on the site.

Granada, North Cheam, pictured in October 1937. It opened three weeks before, showing Fred Astaire & Ginger Rogers in "Shall we dance?". The cinema seated 2,000 people, had a mighty Wurlitzer organ, and boasted that its patrons would breathe air "laundered in a synthetic mountain stream".

Love Lane, St. Helier, looking south-west. This photograph is another taken by Dr. Peatling. The carter is possibly a rag & bone man. On the right is a Croydon Rural District Council boundary stone, marking the boundary between Carshalton on the left and Morden on the right.

Gypsies in Denmark Road, Carshalton. This is one of the photographs taken by the Carshalton local historian, Dr. A. V. Peatling, sometime before 1922.

Hobden & Carter's furniture van, c.1905. This photograph was probably taken outside the back entrance of 4 Dibbins' Cottages, London Road, Hackbridge, the home of Mr. J. I. Stimpson, the driver of the cart. The address of the firm was London Road, Hackbridge. One of their advertisements in a contemporary Pile's Directory for Wallington reads: "dairy farmers, carriage proprietors and household removers, Hackbridge – our own Pantechnicons used. Superior rubber-tyred carriages on hire. Wedding carriages a speciality. New milk fresh twice daily. A choice herd of 45 cows kept."

Policemen, Carshalton Police Station. Presumably the pressure of work was less then!

Pound Street, Carshalton, in about 1910. Behind the lamp-post, on the corner of West Street, stands the Police Station. It was demolished in 1920, and Carshalton came under the auspices of Wallington Police Station.
On the extreme left of the picture is the wall of Carshalton House.

The shop of French & Co., photographers, Railway Terrace, Wallington, decorated for the coronation of Edward VII in 1902. The little girl in the doorway is Mary French Kempsell, the daughter of H. J. Kempsell, the proprietor.

Thrush's shop, 3 Nightingale Road, Carshalton. This part of Wrythe Green was known as Sopp's corner, after Mr. Sopp who kept the dairy next to this shop, and grazed cows on Wrythe Green. Mrs. Thrush was Mr. Sopp's sister.

Cheam Park House from the south-west, 1928. Running from left to right in the foreground is a ha-ha, or sunken fence, which prevented animals from getting into the garden without interrupting the view. The house, an early 19th century building, stood in Cheam Park until 1944, when it was destroyed by a flying bomb.

Miss Susan Wallace's house, Pound Street, Carshalton, from the west, taken after her death in 1909. The house stood in extensive grounds opposite Carshalton House. The Wallace family were doctors in Carshalton for many years in the 1800s. A note on the back of the photograph identifies the people as General Wallace, Major Wallace and Mrs. Hall.

Harvest Time, Stafford Road, Wallington

Stammers & Field Wallington.

Rural scenes in Wallington around the turn of the century. The location of the photograph above is New Barn Farm, later the site of Croydon Airport.

Ploughing at Wallington.

Lavender cutters, Carshalton. Lavender had been grown locally on a large scale since the 18th century, though production had largely ceased by the early years of this century.

Carshalton Lavender Fields. A Group of Lavender Cutters.

Downs Road, Belmont.   6950.B.Bros.C.

Cottages in Downs Road, Belmont, in about 1900. The entrance to the California car park now occupies the site off the left of the picture. The pit behind the cottages is no longer there, and blocks of flats now occupy the site.

Royal Female Orphanage fête, in the late 1930s. The Orphanage occupied Beddington House (Carew Manor) from 1866 until the outbreak of the Second World War. The caps and shoulder capes worn by the senior girls are particularly distinctive.

The Duchess of Teck at the Royal Female Orphanage in about 1890. In 1893 the Duchess, who had been Princess Mary of Cambridge, became the mother-in-law of the future George V. She died in 1897. Later, George V was patron of the Orphanage, and Queen Mary visited it in 1919.

High Street, Sutton, about 1900. On the right stands the Greyhound Hotel, whose sign-board hangs from the beam across the street. Gower and Company's Ladies' Tailor's shop stood on the corner of Manor Lane.

Carshalton Ponds early this century. The animals are presumably from a passing circus. Close scrutiny reveals two camels amongst the elephants.

All Saints Church is in the background, and next to it, the white building is Queen's Well House, which was demolished to make way for flatlets for elderly people.

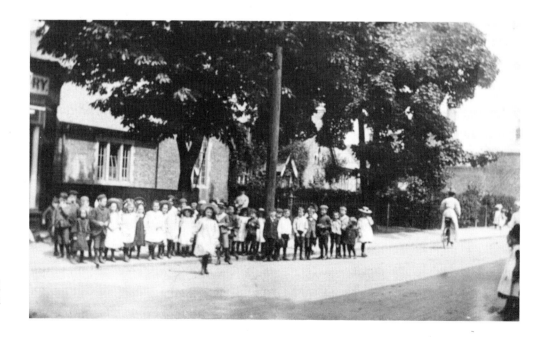

Pupils outside West Street Schools, Sutton, about 1908. The school opened in 1854 and closed in 1968. An open-air market is held on the site of the building.

Herrington's furnishing stores, High Street, Sutton, c.1910. These shops are in the parade between Marshalls Road and Elm Grove. Herrington's also had a menswear and pawnbroker's shop at 99 High Street.

One of a series of photographs taken in 1865 by W. Lewis Hind. This is Mr. Potter's butcher's shop, at the entrance to Sutton Gas Works. Eagle Star House now stands on the site.

High Street, Carshalton, in 1928, looking west towards All Saints Church. On the right is Haydon's butcher's shop, on the left the King's Arms. Both buildings were destroyed by bombs in the Second World War. The railings on the left prevent passers-by from falling into the stream which flows into Carshalton Ponds. The stream was culverted in the early 1930s.

The first Carshalton Gas Works, Wrythe Lane, on or near the site of the present gas holder. No details are known of the couple posing with the dog and jug, but they certainly add charm to their surroundings.

Woodcote House, Wrythe Green, in about 1910–20, when it was known as Bedford Cottage, a name later applied to part of it. With an unusual herringbone timber cladding, it is said to have been a toll house at Rose Hill, and to have been transported to its present position on rollers. It has been greatly restored and rebuilt over the last decade. The weather-vane is now in the Victoria & Albert Museum.

The Queen's Head, Mitcham Junction, c.1890. This attractively posed picture shows the eighteenth century weatherboarded pub which was replaced early this century by the present building.

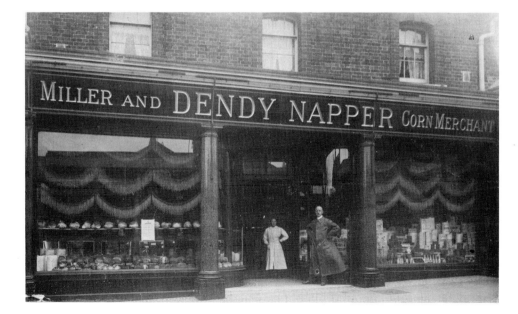

Dendy Napper's shop, High Street, Sutton. In the window, above the loaves, hang three rows of ears of grain: wheat, oats and barley, which were renewed each year. The building had previously been the Police Station, and is now Lilley & Skinner.

The shop of G. J. Millest, grocer, 1 Railway Approach, Wallington, in c.1910. Mr. Millest was one of the principal grocers in the area, who served Wallington residents for many years from the 1890s onwards. The shop is no longer in existence: the site is part of the current development around Wallington station.

The official opening of Trinity Church, Cheam Road, Sutton, in 1908. This photograph was produced from one of the Knights Whittome glass negatives.

Woodcote Road, Wallington, in 1908. The shops on the left include Riddington's the baker's and Noble's the chemist's. The pace, both of pedestrians and traffic, is obviously leisurely.

Woodcote Road, Wallington, c.1930. A similar view to the one above, with many of the shops the same as in the earlier photograph. The houses behind the wall on the left gradually disappeared in the 1930s, to be replaced by shops. The road and railway bridge were widened in the 1960s.

Old and new Red Lion Public Houses, High Street, Sutton, 1907. The new pub, on the right, was completed before the old building, to the left, was pulled down.

Corner of High Street and Cheam Road, Sutton, c.1900. The London Provincial Bank, which later became Barclays, was built in 1894. The Railway Tavern, on the left, was succeeded by The Green Man.

Queen's Well, Carshalton, in 1899. It was probably an 18th century building incorporating an earlier house. It stood next to All Saints Church until it was demolished in the mid 1960s. Anne Boleyn's Well, from which the house took its name, is marked by the railings on the left.

All Saints Church and Anne **Boleyn's Well**, Carshalton, 1928. The doorway on the corner of the churchyard, to the right of the little Morgan car, once led to the engine-house, built in 1836, where the fire pump was kept. It was in use until the Fire Station in Pound Street was built in 1867.

An early photograph of Mount Pleasant, the cottages which still stand at the end of Bridges Lane, Beddington. Access to the front doors can only be achieved by the footbridge. The footpath leads to Beddington Lane. On the left behind the trees, the chimneys of Wandle Court, the home of the Tritton family, can be seen and, on the left of the footpath, its 18th century wall.

The Fords, Beddington, looking towards Beddington Lane. The wall of Wandle Court can be seen on the right. The building in the centre, beyond the trees, is the house belonging to the owner of Beddington Mill, just rebuilt when this picture was taken, whose roof can be glimpsed behind the trees, centre. Next to the house, two millstones lean against an outbuilding.

The Paragon, 112 High Street, Sutton, in 1957. This shop, a well-known local landmark, was demolished in 1960 so that the footpath could be widened. A new shop front was erected in line with its neighbours, and this is now occupied (1981) by the Sutton Cobbler.